'The river Roth⌐
rove'.
One of Northia⌐
Rother or Limen,
as the back door
Sussex from Kent. ⌐ne present oriage, commonly known as Newenden Bridge, was built in 1706. Records show that there has been some sort of structure over the river for several centuries.

An oil painting of the Rother.

Goods were delivered by boat to Newenden as late as 1900. This photo shows coal being unloaded on the Northiam side of the river. In 1815 goods were delivered to Northiam from London by the boat *Mary Ann*. It is not certain whether Captain Cooper brought his boat up to Newenden or discharged his cargo at Rye so that it could be transferred by wagon to Northiam.

During the 1920s local residents enjoyed their recreation on the River Rother.

The road between the bridge and the railway line is known as the 'Ferry'. It may be that at one time a ferry was needed to travel the distance between Northiam and Newenden. The road rarely floods nowadays but Grandfather could remember rowing a boat across on a similar occasion.

In the 1890s the suggestion of a railway through Northiam was discussed. A meeting was arranged at Maytham Hall, Rolvenden, to advocate the continuation of the line from Hawkhurst to Appledore. Mr James Moreton Lord accompanied his father, Mr James Winser Lord of Church House, Northiam, to the meeting and put forward his father's suggestion that the line should run from Strawberry Hole to Robertsbridge. This created an uproar but nevertheless it was decided that Mr Lord and Mr Holman F. Stephens should walk this proposed route to Robertsbridge. This completed, Mr Stephens returned to Tonbridge by goods train and Mr Lord set out again for Northiam. As the snow was starting to fall he was very relieved to be met by his father at Vinehall. This is how the railway came into existence in April 1900. For the first four years it ran between Robertsbridge and Rolvenden and was called the 'Rother Valley Railway'. The line was then extended to Headcorn and became known as the 'Kent and East Sussex Railway'. The return ticket to London cost 5/- (25p) return. It was not unknown for the train to return for a passenger who had just missed it!

The small cottage next to the level crossing has now been demolished to make way for a more modern chalet bungalow.

Some of the engines were named after the villages along the route. This is the 'Northiam'.

The opening of the railway line led to the development of this end of the parish to the extent of forming a cattle market, building an hotel, cottages and a roller mill. Mr Charles J. Banister built and then extended the roller mills shown in these two photographs. He installed roller mill machinery run by gas engines and ended up having one of the most up-to-date plants in the country. In 1910 he entered and won a competition at the London Bakers and Confectioners Exhibition for the best sample of flour from English wheat. He was successful in both the next two years and became the outright owner of the Cup.

Gate Court is first mentioned in records of 1235. In 1284 the owner was John Atte Gate whose seal was a shield with three gates. He died in 1308 leaving the Manor to his son.

In the sixteenth century Lord Windsor owned both Gate Court and Great Dixter. This house claims to be the only house in Northiam used continuously as a farmhouse since these early times.

The hill from the Station, named after a local inhabitant and known as Ballards Hill, was part of the turnpike road. During the sixteenth century James Wilford, a Rippier from Rye, travelled to London through Northiam with fish in panniers and returned as a general carrier. He claimed to have made the road from River Hill to Northiam Church and in his Will of 1514 left an annuity of £7 for its perpetual repair, chargeable upon property belonging to the Merchant Taylors Company and payable upon notice that such road was in need of repair. It is recorded that he directed the money should be paid to the Executor and relatives bearing the name of Wilford and after their death to the Vicar and Churchwardens of Rye. Should they omit to do their duty it was to be paid to the Vicar and Churchwardens of Northiam and failing that to Newenden. However all three parishes failed to claim and the money accumulated for twenty years. All three then claimed and the money was paid to Rye. They handed it to the Trustees of the Turnpike Road from Flimwell to Rye who, in turn, transferred it to the Kent County Council. The annuity has now lapsed and the Kent County Archivist can find no record of James Wilford and his £7!

In 1751 Doctor Burton, a Professor of Greek at Oxford, who visited his relations 'in this muddy, fertile spot', found 'the impassible Sussex roads'. He is also responsible for the statement that the people he saw on the journey were 'long legged because they stretched their muscles so frequently in pulling their feet out of the mud'.

Sometimes a whole summer was not dry enough to make the road passable and it is said that as many as 22 oxen were required to draw one tree. The Sussex oxen were red. Having horns, they were difficult to shoe as they all had to be thrown, their necks held by a pitchfork and their feet tied together.

Gatecourt Farm.

3

The northern end of the Station road was a much more lonely place than it is now with only two or three houses along its length. Osbourne Cottages can be seen on the right-hand side of the photograph.

This thatched cottage was formerly called Ken Bull.

The Workhouse Cottages were called the House of Industry and latterly named Knelle View Terrace. At one time there were five cottages and a bakehouse. When used as a poorhouse these buildings housed as many as ninety-two people. In 1835 the institution was taken over by the Rye Union Authority and inventories were taken. The houses were probably in use for about one hundred years prior to this date. Two cottages and the bakehouse were demolished leaving the three shown in the picture. These were replaced by three pairs of semi-detached houses in 1966.

Two bungalows now stand on the site of Myrtle Cottage, one reputedly built over its well!

Chestnut Cottage, a timber framed cottage, stood on the site of the present Fish and Chip shop.

Marlows was once a row of four cottages which took its name from a previous owner who was a Carrier. Marlows was a part of seven acres called Ryders. This area of Northiam was in the Borough of Purifield which belonged to the Manor of Robertsbridge. A borough consisted of ten freeholders, who, with their families, gave a pledge of good conduct with each other.

The Manor of Robertsbridge was divided into five 'Borowes' for rental purposes. They were:

i) Robertsbridge.
ii) Farlegh — parts of Fairlight, Guestling and Westfield.
iii) Hodlegh — Brightling, Dallington, Burwash, Mayfield and Ticehurst.
iv) Peryfield or Purifield in Northiam.
v) Stretfield — which included other parts of Northiam and Ewhurst.

Reed Pond Cottages were once known as the Black Bull, which was licenced to sell beer. It also boasted a skittle alley.

The smallest house in Sussex was last occupied about eighty years ago by a tenant who smoked opium! The accommodation is as follows: Back and front doors. Pantry. Cupboard. Living room with fireplace. Stairs. Bedroom. A six foot man, his wife and three children were known to have lived here.

Japonica Cottage is still recognisable from this picture although now much altered and extended.

5

Turnpike Cottage, then known as Clench Green Cottage, was bought for £200 on 25th March 1922, with a down payment of £50 and interest at 5%.

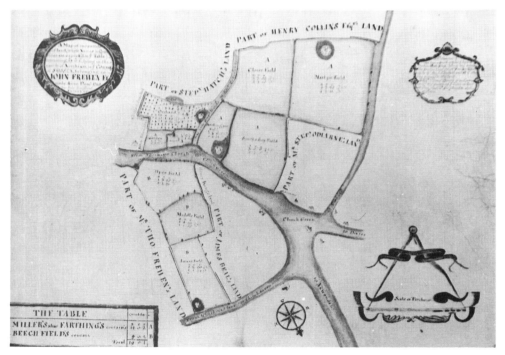

The junction of Beales Lane and the main road used to be called Cuckold Corner. This map of 1729 clearly shows Clench Green.

Beales Lane Cottage was once a pair of semi detached cottages with a third cottage standing in the garden. This rejoiced in the name of Lot's Castle.

This view looking north shows Dora Cottage and Turnpike Cottage on the left. On the right is Clench Green Cottage followed by Lawn Cottage. The next building has been altered out of recognition and now comprises Jessamine House, Forge Cottage, the estate agent's shop, Men's Club and Library. Rosebud, Dora Cottage and Turnpike Cottage can be seen in the background. Compare this photo with the one following.

This Spanish oak was planted at the bottom of the top green by Mrs James Winser Lord in 1902 for the Coronation of Edward VII.

Several commemorative trees stand on the village green, the most well documented being the Queen Elizabeth Oak. Even in 1587 it was termed the 'great old oak'. On 28th March 1884 a committee was appointed to fence it in and on 24th March 1887 another committee was formed to inspect the Elizabeth Oak and to decide on what steps were to be taken, if any, for the preservation of the tree. To have actually been such a mature tree in the sixteenth century it may well have been grown from an acorn planted as long ago as 800 – 900 AD. In 1851 the tree apparently measured 24 feet in circumference one yard above the ground.

In a book written by Moreton Frewen he tells us that in 1904 he collected 20 acorns from the Elizabeth Oak. Ten of them went to Sandringham to be planted by King Edward. The other ten went to the White House where they were planted by President Roosevelt. He adds that the most promising of the ten is the one at Brede, on the village green. Presumably this is the one close to the church.

The smaller oak next to the Elizabeth Oak is a tree planted by Mrs Piper of Strawberry Hole to commemorate Queen Victoria's Golden Jubilee in 1887. The larger oak next to it is supposedly grown from an acorn of the old oak.

In front of the Six Bells is an oak planted for the Coronation of George V. This was planted by Mrs A. Holmes of Tufton Place in 1911.

This Peace Oak was donated by the Rev. Basil Smythe and planted by the Georges and Elizabeths in the village to celebrate the end of World War II. Unfortunately it did not survive.

The two cottages opposite the Queen's Oak were pulled down around 1900 and the present pair erected.

Pheasants hanging outside the butcher's shop towards the end of the last century. The building is now the craft shop.

The village pump was presented to the village by a Miss Margesson who lived at the Hayes. The photographs show the opening ceremony in May 1907.

It is inscribed 'As a grateful thank offering this well in presented to the villagers of Northiam. May 1907 E.C.M.

'And let him that is athirst come, and whosoever will, let him take the water of life freely.' Rev.22:17'.

The crowds at the opening ceremony.

The Northiam War Memorial was designed by Sir Guy Dawber with a stone base, oak columns and a statue of St George and the Dragon to form the capital. It was erected in 1921 at a cost of £400.

'Your lot the glorious price to pay
Ours to record with grateful pride
That freedom lives on earth today
Because you died.'

A. Frewen Aylward, Rector of Northiam, 1914 – 1933

Fair days were held on the village green, first on the upper green, shown here, and later on the lower green by the Six Bells, as shown below.

The Northiam Delicatessen was once a cottage and a dressmaker's shop.

The cottages on the right of the entrance to Hayes Farm have long since been demolished.

T. COPPINGER,
SIX-BELLS INN,
Northiam.

	£.	s.	d.
Breakfast			
Lunch	—	3	8
Dinner	—	17	.
Wine		7	6
Tobacco			6
Tea...................			
Coffee.................			
Supper			
Punch			
Ale	—	—	6
Bottle Porter...........			
Porter	—	2	6
Negus.................	—	2	
Spirits			
Spirits mixed...........	—	7	6
Cider			
Lodging...............			
Servants' Eating			
Corn			
Hay			
Firing			
Washing...............			
Paper.................			
Servant	2	1/2	2
	1	—	
£	1	3	2

Taylor, Printer, Rye.

The bill for £1.3s.2d represents the account for Wm Perigoe when making an inventory of the Poorhouse, Northiam, on 25th and 26th November 1835.

Six Bells Hotel from Village Green, Northiam

The Six Bells Hotel is seen in a series of pictures, the earliest dating from about 1870, the others from the early 1900s until the late 1940s.

The principal family resident in Northiam during the sixteenth century and the first half of the seventeenth century was the White family of Brickwall. In 1491 Thomas White of Rye purchased the house and forty acres of adjoining land. We are told that the earliest deed in which the name Brickwall House is mentioned is dated 8th September 1615. William White, a descendant of Thomas, altered the house by putting on a new front with three gables. The western one was erected in 1617, the centre in 1633 followed by the eastern one. Initials and date on the bressemer read W.M.W. 1633. William White died at Northiam on 6th April 1666. The estate was then sold to Stephen Frewen, son of John Frewen of Church House, Alderman of the City of London and Master of the Skinners Company. In addition to the house, the property included 652 acres in Northiam, Beckley and Brede, the purchase price being £4,189. Stephen Frewen is reputed to have had his own coffin in his bedroom for some years before his death in 1679 in order, as he said, to familiarise himself with death!

In 1752 a tragedy occurred at this house when Martha, wife of Thomas Frewen, was burned to death in her bedroom. The discovery was made by the passengers on the coach from Rye to London who, on hearing her screams, went to investigate. The sedan chair in which the lady used to be carried is still at Brickwall. In 1835 Thomas Frewen moved the road further away from the front of the house. He also erected wrought iron entrance gates. In 1838 a wall was built along the Hastings road. The date and initials are built in with bricks of a different colour. In 1863 the park was enlarged, thereby enclosing the old road opposite Perryman's Cross. Another was cut a little further south from Road End, Beckley, to Umbersome, Northiam. This was called the 'New Road', a name by which it is still known today. An avenue of Spanish Chestnuts was also planted through the park.

The park, at one time, contained a herd of 18 red, 35 fallow and 9 japanese deer. In the warren area were several crested cranes, a marabou stork, adjutant bird, spur winged goose, a pair of gazelles and some Australian wallabies. (The following birds are known to have been shot on the estate: honey buzzard 1909, common buzzard, peregrine falcon, bittern grey phalarone and lesser spotted woodpecker.)

The Wilderness in 1810.

21

Great Stent Farm is an interesting property on the Northiam border. When renovations were taking place about thirty years ago it was discovered that the weatherboarding was covering a wealth of old timbers. A small window, containing its original glass, was found. This had probably been covered up when windows were subjected to tax. In 1695 houses were permitted six windows free of tax. This tax was increased six times until 1815. It was eventually repealed in 1851.

The Northiam/Beckley boundary passes through this farmhouse. When Benjamin Broomfield died here in a bedroom on the Northiam side double burial fees had to be paid as he wished to be buried in Beckley!

The flower show was held in Brickwall Park in 1909 and was attended by 4,000 people. It is noted that a half marathon was run, ending, it is believed, in the Pretious field.

Yew Tree Farm, or Mary Masons, is another fourteenth century Northiam house. It has a rare 'pink' tiled floor. Similar tiles can be seen in the crypt of St Paul's. The iron and the tiles for the original St Paul's which was destroyed in the Great Fire of London were produced in the vicinity.

During the war a large photograph of this house appeared on the front page of SEAC, the journal of the South East Asia Command, as a symbol of 'Home'.

Another view of the toll cottage, Horns Cross.

There is no longer a toll cottage at the junction of the Horn Cross/Brede, Horns Cross, Staplehurst roads. With today's volume of traffic it would hardly be wise for the Hunt to meet there. The last occupant was Mrs Alice Selmes, who was in residence up until 1938.

In 1929 the authoress, Sheila Kaye-Smith, and her husband, Mr Penrose-Fry, completed the alterations to Little Doucegrove, which was once an oasthouse. Mr and Mrs Fry were also responsible for building the Roman Catholic Church in Northiam. This was opened in December 1935 and dedicated to St Theresa of Lisieux.

Doucegrove, not pictured here, is another of Northiam's really old properties. It takes its name from Robert Douce (pronounced Dooce), a French Huguenot, who came to give instruction in the iron trade. He married a local girl and changed the pronunciation of his name to Dowse.

The following description of Tan House was taken from a sale catalogue of 1926. 'The Genuine Old Farm House is reputed to date in parts from the XV century, being of brick, weatherboarded, half timbered and tile construction, and standing well back from the road. It contains a wealth of old oak, visible in the floors, beams and walls. The accommodation comprises hall, sitting room with beamed ceiling and deeply recessed hearth, Jacobean oak panelled dining room, morning room, kitchen, larder and dairy. An oak staircase leads to five bedrooms and there are two garrets above.'

In the eighteenth century this home belonged to the Haddock family of Rye who used it as their summer residence. The Haddocks were devoted Methodists and opened up the house for preaching about 1745. It was used for this purpose until 1845. It is reported that John Wesley visited here on several occasions and services were later taken by the Rev. Thomas Collins in the room called the hall.

The story really starts with Ann Barnes who was a wealthy and devout member of the Rye Methodist Society. When Capt. Henry Haddock fell in love and subsequently proposed to her he was turned down on account of being a Church man. However he started to attend the Methodist services and was converted. Miss Barnes now accepted his proposal but her happiness was shortlived! Capt. Haddock, whilst commanding his vessel between Dover and Dunkirk, spied a smuggling craft. He ordered his men not to fire; they did and the smugglers then retaliated with their big guns. Capt. Haddock was hit and died almost immediately in the arms of one of his crew. This was in August 1783 when he was only 18 years old. The name of the sailor was David

Manser, who lived in Northiam until 1845. This event so upset Capt. Haddock's brother, John, that he also started to attend the Methodist Society. He, too, fell in love with his widowed sister-in-law and they were happily married on 12th June 1786. Her dowry consisted of her weight in gold! During his short life John built the chapel and minister's house in Rye at his own expense. John died on 15th November 1797 after venturing to save some sailors shipwrecked near Rye.

Four years later Mrs Haddock married again. This time to another Methodist who was a preacher and class leader.

Interesting details of the family life at Tanhouse were told some years ago by Colin Bridger who died in 1904 in his ninetieth year. He lived in Tanhouse as a lad with his grandfather, Henry Bridger, who was the farm manager. The winter months were spent in their house in Rye, now Adams Shop, and the summer at Tanhouse. Farm wagons would be sent to Rye for the servants and furniture, the return journey being made in the same way. Mrs Haddock used a newly painted farm cart for her journey, being nervous of any other mode of transport.

About 100 years ago, when repairs were being done and alterations made to the fireplace in the large sitting room, two doors were found. These opened to reveal a brass coining stove with two brass ovens. This was given to the Hastings Museum by Mr John Barnett, the tenant at the time. Around the same time a hidden room was also discovered leading out of the chimney to the fireplace in the adjoining room. It is said that interesting articles were found here, which were also presented to the museum. For those interested in the occult, this house is known to be haunted.

Well House is a fine example of a fourteenth century house with a hall still open to the roof. A fresco discovered in the dining room represented the Tree of Life. At one time Well House was the keeper's house for the Brickwall estate. The staghounds met here for the last time in 1874 and later the foxhounds were kept in kennels on the east side.

Susser National Society,
FOR THE
EDUCATION OF THE POOR.

THE GENERAL COMMITTEE for the EASTERN DIVISION of this County, conceiving that the Advantages of the improved Mode of Instruction have not been well understood, deem it proper to make this public Explanation of their Object and Intentions, and to request the early aid of those, who may approve of the Plan.

It is proposed to recommend the immediate Establishment of a SCHOOL in every Town and Village throughout the County, where the Children of the Poor shall be taught Reading, Writing, and Arithmetic, by the *new* mode of Education, and be instructed in the Principles of Religion, according to the *Established Church*.

The Advantages, to be derived from the improved Plan of teaching, arise from the considerable Saving to be made, both in the Expense, and Time necessary for acquiring Instruction.

I. By appointing to each Class in the School, one or two (and sometimes more) of the best Scholars in that Class, to teach the others, under the Direction of the Master.

II. By employing various short Words of Command or Signals, by which ORDER is easily maintained, the Attention of the Scholar kept up, and the whole Proceedings of a large Number rendered uniform and expeditious.

III. By teaching the Children to read and write at the same Time, by the use of Sand and Slates, and Printed Lessons hung on the walls of the School, and thus reducing the Expense of Paper, Pens, and Books.

IV. By encouraging the Scholars to observe the Rules laid down as to Cleanliness and Order, and to learn their Lessons by *Rewards and Distinctions*.

N. B. For a small Sum, a Master or Mistress may be instructed in the *new* Mode of teaching, by attending for a short Time, any large School formed on this Plan.

The *General Committee*, in offering this short Explanation of the *new* Mode of Education, beg to call the Attention of the Inhabitants of the several Towns and Villages in this District, where it has not been adopted, to the Simplicity of the Plan, and its tried Utility; assuring them, on their own Parts, that they will be ready, at all Times, to give every Information and Assistance in their Power, either in the Formation of new Schools, or in the Improvement of those already established.

Applications are requested to be directed to the *Secretary*, the Rev. JOHN LUPTON, Ringmer, Lewes.

Lewes: Printed by W. and A. Lee.

Rev. W. Lord built the school, at his own expense, in 1844. It was enlarged in 1888 and again in 1914.

Letters used to be posted at the Rosary. They were dropped, from outside, into a cupboard in the chimney corner. The shop was once a grocer's.

The Grove, just out of view on the right, was used as a small school. Mrs Elphick, the schoolmistress, kept white mice which used to run all over the schoolroom.

Carriers Farm. It is said that there was once an underground passage leading from Carriers to Brickwall!?

Carriers was the first home in Northiam of the Frewen family. John Frewen moved here from Worcestershire in 1583, having been presented to the living by his father, Richard. It was at Carriers that John's eldest son, Accepted, was born. Accepted was Archbishop of York from 1660 to 1664.

CARRIERS FARM

The windmill at High Park was built in 1806 on the site of another mill which had been destroyed by fire. This mill ceased working around 1910 and was finally pulled down in 1949.

The mill and the cottage in the background were said to be the haunts of smugglers as were Thornton House, Waites Wood and the Little House.

Great Dixter is regarded as one of the most important and perhaps the earliest timber house in Sussex. There was an Adam de Dyksters in 1295 and in 1340 Hamo at Gate was liable to find one man-at-arms in respect of his land at Dicksterve. Hamo's daughter married Robert Etchingham and the house stayed in their possession until the late fifteenth century when it passed to the Windsor family with whom it remained until 1595. The Windsors leased Dixter to the father of John Harrison who, in 1595 or thereabouts, scratched the following inscription on the beam of the parlour: 'John Harrison dwelt att Dixter xxxvi yers an vi monthes, came ye ferst of Elizabethe rain'.

It is a probable theory that when John Harrison died or left Dixter in 1595 the new owner, John Glydd, remodelled the house, built the great chimney and divided the open hall into three storeys.

During the eighteenth and nineteenth centuries Great Dixter was owned by the Springetts, a family who can trace their ancestry back to the thirteenth century and whose descendants own property in the village today.

At some time they were owners of many properties both locally and in the Kent/Sussex area. Coplands, Coplands Cottage, and Church Green Cottages in Northiam, Boakes Farm in Hawkhurst, Finchcocks, Goudhurst and Ringmer Place to name a few.

The alliances of the family are of particular interest. In 1672 Gulielma Maria Springett (1644 – 1693), the daughter of Sir William Springett, married William Penn (1644 – 1718) founder of Pennsylvania.

A century later Elizabeth Springett married Samuel Boys of Elfords, Hawkhurst. The romance of their daughter, Elizabeth with Charles Lamb is told in detail by Geoff Hutchinson in his book 'The Lovers' Seat, Fairlight Glen'.

Eventually Great Dixter passed into the hands of Mr Nathaniel Lloyd who, together with the architect Edwin Lutyens, restored and extended the house. 'The old house at home', a general shop with a licence to sell beer, was moved from Benenden and embodied in the alterations.

Watering the horses at Great Dixter Pond.

During the 1914–1918 war Great Dixter was lent by Mr Lloyd to accommodate French and Belgian refugees. Following this it became a convalescent home for British soldiers.

During the war it was staffed entirely by VAD members from Northiam. On 18th March 1935 Queen Mary paid a visit to Great Dixter.

An old map shows that a road once ran from Northiam by way of Little Dixter to Padgham, in the parish of Ewhurst. Tradition says that Little Dixter was an inn. Centuries ago Padgham was a sea port.

Before there was any such thing as a National Health Service or any form of insurance scheme against ill health or injury the residents of the Sussex villages clubbed together to form their own friendly society or club and were thus able to help those suffering undue hardship through ill health, injury or old age.

Club Days were held in Northiam on the first Thursday in May. All members had to wear white smocks, called 'round frocks'. these were called 'emblems of purity' by the late Mr James Winser Lord. Club members paraded to church, through the street, up around the hill past the windmill and back to the Crown and Thistle for a bread and cheese lunch — the mid-morning break on the way to the village green for a mid-day meal in a booth. The day ended with coconut shies, swing boats and refreshments such as gingerbread and oval cakes. My own great grandfather, and great, great grandfather took part in these parades.

These clubs began to lose importance once more general health insurance became available.

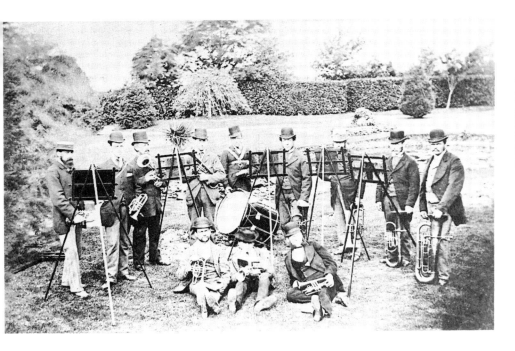

The Northiam Brass Band was formed by Mr Alfred Comport in 1873. This earliest photo shows them rehearsing in the grounds of Elmside. The uniforms were originally navy blue with red and gold trimming. After the war this altered to navy blue and blue. By this time the band had also 'gone silver'.

This photo includes Messrs Crouch, Dengate, Ballard, Poile, Bob and Harry Playford.

Northiam Band in the playing fields.
Left to right, back row,
standing: Jim Padgham, Reg Pattenden.
sitting: Bert Jarman – band leader/conductor, Bert Polhill, Ted Firrell, ??, Ernie Offin, Ted Dunk, Jack Jarman, George Bryant, Jim Lockyer, Bert Marchant, Bob Playford, Jack Padgham, George Bates, Charlie Harman, Norman Carter.

A Church Parade

In 1821 a resolution was passed to value and map the parish, showing all properties and who owned and lived in them at the time. On 4th May 1826 the boundary between Northiam and Beckley was walked by the two rectors and the inhabitants of the two parishes and two maps were drawn up by common consent and one map deposited in the chest of each parish.

In the survey of John Adams of Tenterden every property, every field and every cottage is set down with exact areas, situation and names of the owners and occupiers.

Following this the usual custom of 'Beating the Bounds' took place, the last time being on 14th April 1902.

The photograph shows one of the last beating of the bounds and was probably taken around 1900 – 1902.

Haymaking

38

Hop Picking. Tusser wrote in 1557:
  'get into thy hop-yard
  for now it is time
  To teach Robin Hop on
  His pole to climb'

Hop growing and picking was very much an integral part of life in the local villages as can be seen from the family groups in these photos.

Payment to pickers was often made in tallies, thus accounting for the number of bushels picked. These would be redeemed later. The photo shows one of James Hodges' tallies dated 1856.

Taking a sample of the hops.

Mobile wheelwright

Thatching

Charcoal burning

Bicycle parades were once a popular event.

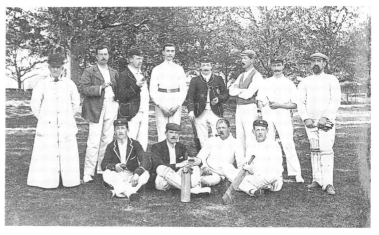

Excerpts from newspapers read as follows:

3rd September 1822

A Match of Cricket was played on Benenden Green on Saturday the 24th ultimo, between the gentlemen of Benenden and the gentlemen of Sandhurst, Bodiam, Northiam, Beckley and Rye, for five guineas, which owing to the night coming on, was not played out, but the game was given in favour of the Benenden gentlemen.

and again

19th August 1828

On Thursday a Match of Cricket was played at Northiam, between the gentlemen of that place and the gentlemen of Appledore; the former beat their opponents to the amount of 70 runs and upwards. There was much scientific play on the part of the Northiam players, among whom were Gladwish and Bowley, they being the admiration of the whole field.

The only member of this team known is Charles Banister. He is on the right in the front row.

Men's team.
Back row, left to right: ?, ?, Mr Close, ?, ?.
Front row: John Dengate, Alfred Comport, Charles Banister, Charlie Dengate, ?, Alfred Comport Jnr.

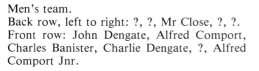

About 1908 a game of cricket was played between the gentlemen and ladies of the parish. The men used broom handles as compensation for the ladies being encumbered by long skirts. When Alice Pix put her foot through her skirt whilst running the umpire had to call for a safety pin!

Ladies team
Left to right,
Back row: Mrs Deane, Mrs C. Dengate, Miss Pix, Miss Jessie Poile, Miss Marsh, Mr Collard.
Front row: ?, Miss Alwin, Miss Kitty Comport, Miss Kitty Close, Miss Parker.

When Mr Moreton Lord bought Crockers Farm in 1900 he inherited a lot of oak trees which he harvested. He was recommended by a timber merchant, Mr Stockdale, with whom he dealt, to plant a variety of willow called *Salix caerulea*. This variety was more suitable for the manufacture of cricket bats than the *Salix alba* as it was more robust.

Mr Lord, in a letter, states that under the most prosperous conditions the sets will measure up to 45″ in circumference, 5′ above the ground after 10 or 11 years. They are ready to fell at 50″ circumference and each tree may produce as many as 40 or 50 clefts. From the few he planted in 1901 thousands of his bats found their way into play not only in this country, but all over the world.

Parts of the tree not used for cricket bats were used for trug making and we know that some of the trugs made from Crockers Wood were exported to New York.

Football still thrives in the village, the first team having been formed over 100 years ago in 1873. The strip was pale blue and chocolate and a gentleman by the name of H.C. Thomas designed the badges.

Col. Frewen's return from the Boer War.

Volunteer Force of the 1914 – 18 War.

Combined Church Parade, Northiam, August 1941, with the 11th Canadian Field Ambulance RCAMQ Canadian Army.

Home Guard from the Second World War.
Back row: George Waters, Mac Piper, Bill Standen, Punch Pearce, Arthur Carter, Jack Sinden, Harold Barnes, ?, ?, Bill Barnes, ?, ?, Bert Catt, Bob Roberts, Jack Tedham.
Middle row: Bert Marchant, Mr Parkes, Ginger Jones, Charlie Addy, Jim Rainton, Les Skinner, Walter Wilson, Peter Edwards, Jack Harris, George Jefferies, Trevor Francis, Fred Batehup, Ernie Sealey, Albert Jones, ?, Bill Unicombe.
Front row: Jim Padgham, Ernie Noakes, Walter Paine, Eddie Shinner, ?, Ken Pattenden, Bill Banister, Frank Bishop, Arthur Boyce, Rupert Cyster, Ted Hinkley, Will Perigoe, Bert Polhill.

VAD 1914 – 1918 at Great Dixter
Left to right,
Back row: Mrs N. Ballard, J. Batram, M. Emerton, D. Aylward, Judy Marchant, Gladys Haynes, Mrs Wenban.
Front row: Mrs Crouch, Miss Masters, G. Wenban, ?, Nellie Perigoe, Miss G. Lord.

The Staff of the Hundred of Staple is 5′2″ in length and 5½″ in diameter. Reddish brown in colour with blue and gold trimmings and in perfect condition.

Hundred was the ancient divisional name given to a portion of a county for administrative and military purposes. They varied in size and were first mentioned in the time of Edgar. It was understood to be the territory occupied by a hundred families, or the space of a hundred hides or to have the capacity to provide one hundred soldiers. The inhabitants were collectively responsible for the maintenance of the peace. Each hundred had its own court with powers similar to those of a manor court. Twice a year a special court was held when the Sheriff attended and criminals were tried. Gradually most of the Hundred courts fell under the control of the Lords of the Manor and from the sixteenth century ceased to have much importance. They were eventually abolished in 1867 by the County Court Act.

Northiam was in the Hundred of Staple. The name taken from the Hamlet of Staple Cross in the parish of Ewhurst which was in the centre of the Hundred. The parishes of Northiam (Hiham), Ewhurst Green (Werste), Bodiam (Bodeham), Sedlescombe (Salescome) were totally within the Hundred of Staple together with parts of the parishes of Brede, Mountfield and Whatlington.

The dictionary definition of a hatchment is a tablet with the deceased person's armorial bearings affixed to the front of his house.

The undertaker's sign is a fairly unusual item. Although there are thousands of hatchments there are only a few dozen of the undertaker's signs.

When hatchments were first used they were supplied by the College of Arms, who had agents, or deputies in various parts of the country. Later, the undertakers cashed in on this monopoly and as they were usually cheaper than the Heralds, captured the major part of the market. On several occasions the Hanoverian Kings were asked to prohibit the undertakers, but took no action. Last century many undertakers showed hatchments in their windows to indicate that they could provide suitable hatchments, if required.

The features of these display hatchments are such that they cannot cause offence. The arms are carefully chosen so that they shall not resemble any genuine coat of arms. The rule of metal on colour is often deliberately broken, so that it shall be obvious that the arms are fictitious. The motto is usually replaced by the words 'Funerals Furnished'.

On this hatchment the coronet is that of a Marquess. The ermine mantling and the supporters are of a type used by many peers. The collar with motto is not that of any existing order and the arms are not listed in Papworth's 'Ordinary of Arms'. The background would be all or part black in a real hatchment.

One or two pieces of china with a picture of Northiam Church, dating from approximately 1840, are still in existence. The design is fluted and decorated in shaded pink and gold on a white background.

Edward and Leah Perigoe with phaeton outside Oak House.

The carrier's carts.

A horse bus

Harry Streeton — the postman.

7 SPACE FLIGHT

PUSHING IN PAIRS
(students' book page 28)

Apparatus: straw; bulldog clip; nylon fishing line; clamps and stands; sausage-shaped balloon; sticky tape; rocket trolley

New words: rocket, bulldog clip, taut, rocket trolley, compressed, carbon dioxide, capsule, Catherine wheel

LIFT-OFF!
(students' book page 29)

Apparatus: clampstand; empty washing-up-liquid bottle; bicycle pump; 2 funnel holders; plastic cap fitted with bicycle tyre valve; beaker

ROCKETS
(students' book page 29)

New words: space, air, oxygen, atmosphere, satellites, orbit

 Handle the rocket trolley with care.

A sausage-shaped balloon is best for this experiment. Also, nylon line reduces friction and makes for a better launch. The balloon is pushed forwards by the push from the air inside the balloon. The balloon, in turn, pushes the air backwards. We therefore have a pair of forces pushing. One force pushes on the balloon and the other pushes on the air inside the balloon.

Q1 The air escapes from the balloon, and the balloon is pushed along the line.

Q3 A force clearly acts on the balloon since it speeds up rapidly from rest.

Q4 The movement of the rocket trolley is explained in terms of forces pushing in pairs. The compressed gas inside the capsule pushes on the capsule, causing it to move forwards. The capsule in turn pushes on the compressed gas, causing it to be pushed backwards out of the capsule. The capsule therefore moves one way and the gas the other. Because the rocket is tethered it moves in a circle.

Q5 A Catherine wheel pushes out burning chemicals. These in turn push back on the Catherine wheel. If the Catherine wheel is fixed it spins. The movement is similar to the rocket trolley.

 This experiment should be done out of doors. Make sure the students keep their heads out of the way of the rocket. Prepare the apparatus beforehand. Glue the bicycle valve into the cap of the bottle. Pump air into the bottle until you have lift-off.

Q1

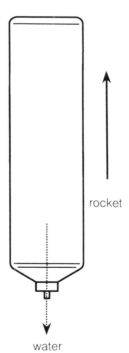

Q2 During the time when the water is being ejected, compressed air pushes upwards on the inside wall of the rocket, causing a high lift-off speed.

Q1 Satellites, lunar modules, space laboratories.

Q2 Rockets have to reach very high speeds to take satellites into orbit. They achieve these high speeds more easily and burn less fuel if air resistance to their motion is reduced. This is done by streamlining rockets.

A PAIR PUSHING!
(students' book page 30)

Apparatus: flat plastic bottle with four holes; thread; paperclip

In this experiment we have more than one pair of forces pushing. The combination of forces on the bottle causes rotation. In this experiment the driving force is produced by water pressure.

Q1 a) In step B, looking from above, the push from the water causes a clockwise motion.
b) Anticlockwise.
c) If the holes are equally spaced, then there will be no rotation. This is because each pair of forces is trying to turn the bottle in opposite directions.

Q2 In step B, for example, we have two forces which produce a clockwise turning effect. These two forces come from the water. The water pushes on the bottle. The bottle, in turn, pushes on the water. The water is pushed one way and the bottle is pushed the other.

Q3 A garden water sprinkler.

MOVEMENT AND THRUST
(students' book page 31)

Apparatus: piece of polystyrene tile 7 cm × 7 cm; 4 'bendy' straws; sticky tape; sheet of A4 paper; scissors; basin of water
New words: thruster rocket, anticlockwise

⚠ Throw away the straws after use.

Use the paper tube as a kind of bearing. Blow down the tube into the straws. Try to direct the air into the straws. The tube will prevent translation of the model and the model will rotate.

Q1 Rotation.
Q2 Bend the straws over so that they face the other way.
Q3 a) We have a pair of forces pushing here, but they are pushing in such a way that they produce neither translation nor rotation.

MOVEMENT IN SPACE
(students' book page 32)

New words: communication, jettison, vacuum, manned manoeuvring unit, nozzle, eject, nitrogen, oxidant

Extension exercise '6 The space shuttle' can be used here.

Q1 Oxidants supply oxygen which is required for fuel to burn. As there is no oxygen in space, rockets need to take supplies with them.

Q2 As each stage drops away there is less mass to be pushed. This way the rocket can speed up more easily. A sufficiently high speed is reached to send the satellite into space and into orbit.

Q3 Firing a set of thruster rockets, one at the top and the other at the bottom, on each side of the unit, will make it roll. For example, the rockets on the top left of the unit, when fired with those on the bottom right, would make the astronaut roll to the right.

RESOURCES

Butterfield, M., *Satellites and Space Stations*, Usborne Publishers, London
McNeil, M. J., *'Know How' Book of Flying Models*, Usborne Publishers, London
Simmons, M., *Airflow*, AE Press, Melbourne

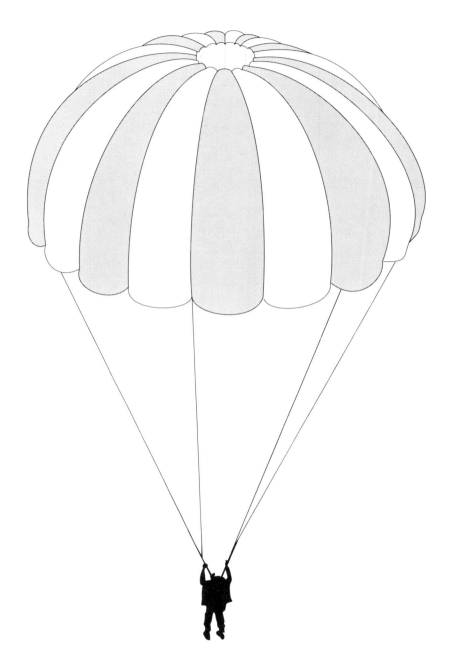

You probably noticed that, during a drop of the parachute you made on page 7 of the students' book, the paperclip swung to and fro. A person making a descent using a parachute like this would not be too comfortable or safe. Umbrella-type parachutes have a central hole cut in their canopy. The hole allows the parachute to let out air and its motion is then more stable. You can put this to the test by cutting a hole in the canopy of a model parachute.

A Cut a hole 2 cm in diameter in the centre of your parachute.

B Drop the chute and compare its motion with a similar parachute without a hole.

Q1 How did the presence of the hole affect the way the parachute fell?

Q2 Find out what happens when you attach a small piece of Plasticine to one of the parachute lines. Try each line in turn.

Q3 If you shorten a line slightly, what effect does this have on the way a parachute falls?

Extends Flight pages 7 and 8

A plastic funnel is held tightly in the neck of a bottle by a rubber bung.

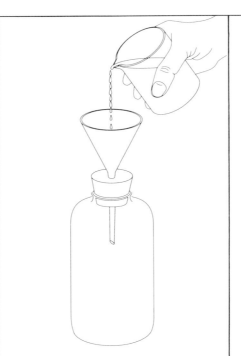

Water is poured into the funnel but does not run down into the bottle.

A straw is gently lowered into the water and down the funnel. Water then runs into the bottle.

Q1 How does this show that the plastic bottle is not empty, but full of air?

Q2 Why does lowering the straw into the funnel cause water to run into the bottle?

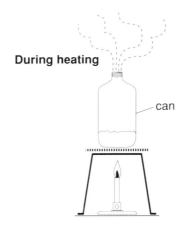

During heating

can

After heating

A can (shown above) was partly filled with water. The can was heated until the water boiled. The can was then sealed and allowed to cool.

Q3 What happened to the air in the can as the water boiled?

Q4 What happened to the water when it was boiled?

Q5 Using the term 'air pressure', explain why the can collapsed.

Extends Flight page 17

Like an aircraft, a bird has to overcome many problems during flight. When a bird flies it has to take off, keep itself stable in the air (balance), overcome air resistance and be able to land. A bird achieves this by movements of its wings, tail and certain feathers. The drawings on page 14 show the side view of a bird during one downstroke and one upstroke of its wings.

A Cut out the pictures on page 14 and arrange them in order.

B Stick the pictures onto cards.

C Put the pictures in a pile (with the first picture on top) and secure them with an elastic band along one side (see the drawing below).

D Flick the cards – if you have the right order you should see the bird flying.

Q1 What is the shape of the wing during a downstroke?

Q2 What is the reason for this shape?

Q3 What is the shape of the wing during an upstroke?

Q4 What is the reason for this?

Q5 The drawings at the bottom of the page show the different positions of the wing feathers during an upstroke and downstroke. What is the reason for the change?

Q6 If you had a supply of bird feathers, how would you show that your answer to Q5 was right?

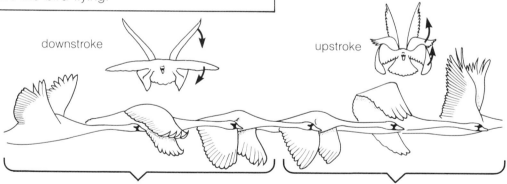

downstroke

upstroke

downstroke – wing pushes against the air, the feathers are overlapped

upstroke – feathers opened up to allow air to pass through

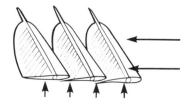

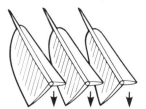

Extends Flight pages 19–20

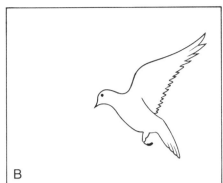

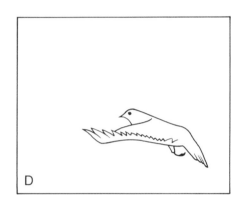

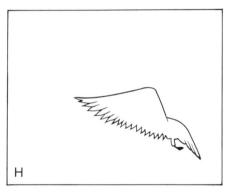

Extends Flight pages 19–20

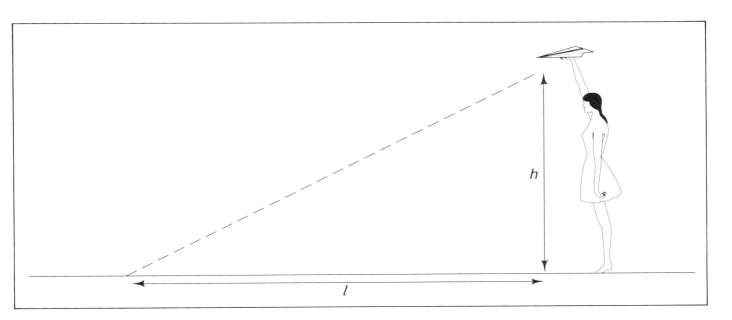

In an experiment eight different types of paper glider were tested and their glide ratios were measured. The glider was thrown from a height (h) of 2 metres and the distance of flight (l) was measured. The table below shows the results for eight different gliders.

$$\text{Glide ratio} = \frac{\text{length of flight}}{\text{height from which the glider is thrown}}$$

Model	l (metres)	h (metres)	Glide ratio l/h
A	20	2	
B	8	2	
C		2	5
D		2	9
E	18	2	
F	16	2	
G	14	2	
H	5	2	

Q1 Copy the table into your book.

Q2 Fill in the blank spaces on the chart.

Q3 Which model had the highest glide ratio?

Q4 Which model had the lowest glide ratio?

Q5 Which models had the same glide ratios?

Q6 Why does the glide ratio have no units?

Q7 Under what conditions must this experiment be carried out if it is to be as reliable as possible?

Q8 What natural conditions might a glider meet which could change its glide ratio?

Extends Flight pages 22–26

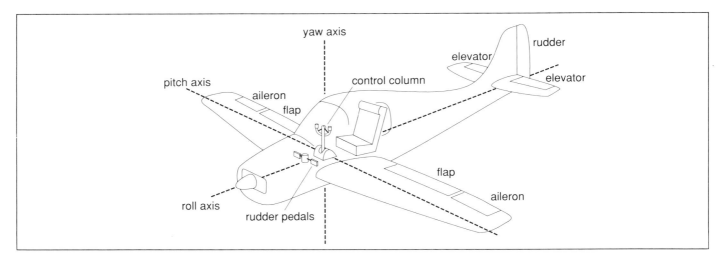

When an aircraft is flying, the body of the plane may pitch, yaw and roll.

Q1 On the drawing above, the pitch, yaw and roll axes are shown. Put arrows on the diagram to show the direction the body could move for each of these movements.

The aircraft has three sets of control surfaces which tilt it about these three axes. These are the rudder on the tail fin, the hinged elevators on the trailing edge of the tail plane, and the ailerons on the wing tips.

Q2 Find the three control surfaces on the drawing above. Colour in each surface you find.

Q3 Which type of movement will the following help to control:
   a) the rudder?
   b) the elevators?
   c) the ailerons?

Q4 The drawing below shows an aircraft in a nose-dive. What must be done to the controls to make the aircraft climb?

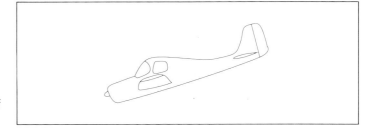

Q5 A delta winged aircraft has no separate tail plane. Which two control surfaces must be combined?

Q6 Look at the drawing below. What name is given to this combined control surface?

Q7 What happens to the combined control surface when the aircraft:
   a) climbs?
   b) banks?
   c) banks and climbs?

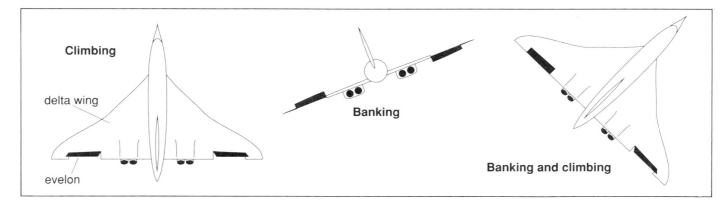